W9-BTL-945

UNITED KINGDOM

Madeline Donaldson

Lerner Publications Company • Minneapolis

Lerner Publications Company
A division of Lerner Publishing Group, Inc.
241 First Avenue North
Minneapolis, MN 55401 U.S.A.

Website address: www.lernerbooks.com

Library of Congress Cataloging-in-Publication Data

Donaldson, Madeline.
    United Kingdom / by Madeline Donaldson.
        p.   cm. — (Country explorers)
    Includes index.
    ISBN 978-0-7613-5315-7 (lib. bdg. : alk. paper)
        1. Great Britain—Juvenile literature. 2. Northern Ireland—
    Juvenile literature. I. Title.
    DA27.5.D66 2011
    941—dc22   2009023178

Manufactured in the United States of America
1 – VI – 7/15/10

Table of Contents

Welcome!

You've made it to the United Kingdom! The United Kingdom is part of the British Isles. These islands lie northwest of Europe. The United Kingdom's largest island is called Great Britain. Another large island is Ireland. Smaller islands dot the seas around Great Britain and Ireland.

Waves crash on the rocky cliffs that line the coast of Great Britain.

SHETLAND
ISLANDS

ORKNEY
ISLANDS

N

OUTER HEBRIDES

INNER HEBRIDES

BEN
NEVIS

SCOTTISH
HIGHLANDS

TAY RIVER

SCOTLAND

FIRTH OF
FORTH

NORTH
SEA

MILES
0   50   100

0   50   100
KILOMETERS

NORTH
ATLANTIC
OCEAN

Glasgow
CLYDE RIVER

★ **Edinburgh**

UNITED KINGDOM

LOWER
BANN
RIVER

SPERRIN
MOUNTAINS

ANTRIM
HILLS

RATHLIN
ISLAND

UPPER
BANN RIVER

LAGAN RIVER

★ **Belfast**

MOURNE
MOUNTAINS

PENNINE MOUNTAINS

OUSE RIVER

Leeds

NORTHERN
IRELAND

IRISH
SEA

Liverpool

Manchester

Sheffield

TRENT RIVER

REPUBLIC
OF
IRELAND

DEE RIVER

SEVERN RIVER

THE FENS
ENGLAND

CAMBRIAN
MOUNTAINS

WALES

Birmingham

London ★

BRISTOL CHANNEL

Cardiff ★

Bristol

THAMES RIVER

EXMOOR

DARTMOOR

ENGLISH CHANNEL

FRANCE

▲ mountains

highlands

★ capital city

• city

Parts of the Kingdom

The United Kingdom's full name is the United Kingdom of Great Britain and Northern Ireland. People often call it Britain for short. The country has four parts. England, Scotland, and Wales are on the island of Great Britain. Northern Ireland sits on the island of Ireland.

The rocky Orkney Islands lie off the northern coast of Scotland.

No part of the United Kingdom is very far from water. Seas lie to the north, east, and west. Rivers and lakes are common in the four parts too.

Map Whiz Quiz

Take a look at the map on page five. A map is a drawing or chart of a place. Trace the outline of the United Kingdom on a sheet of paper. Don't forget Northern Ireland! See if you can find the North Sea. Mark this part of your map with an *E* for east. Find the Irish Sea. Mark it with a *W* for west. The English Channel sits to the south. Mark it with an *S*. In the far north, near Scotland, is the North Atlantic Ocean. Mark it with an *N*. With a green crayon, color the United Kingdom. Color Northern Ireland yellow to show where it ends and the rest of Ireland begins.

Waters of the Bristol Channel wash the shores of Wales near Cardiff.

Ben Nevis in Scotland's Highlands is the highest mountain in the United Kingdom. It is 4,409 feet (1,344 meters) above sea level.

Mountains and Valleys

All four parts of the United Kingdom have mountains and valleys. Ben Nevis is the United Kingdom's highest peak. It's part of Scotland's Highlands. The Pennines range runs from north to south in England. The Cambrian Mountains cover most of Wales. The low Sperrin and Mourne ranges and the Antrim Hills lie in Northern Ireland.

Between the mountains are rolling, green valleys. These give way to coastal lowlands. Most of Britain's people live in the lowlands. The lowlands also hold many of the United Kingdom's major cities.

Giant's Causeway

The Giant's Causeway *(right)* is a landform in Northern Ireland. Millions of years ago, movements took place deep inside Earth. They formed thousands of rock blocks. A legend says a giant used the causeway as a path from Ireland to Scotland.

Cool and Mild

Warm ocean breezes blow inland from Britain's long coastline. These breezes keep the United Kingdom's weather mostly cool and mild. But close to the coasts, the winds can be strong and gusty.

Waves wash the beaches of Wales in the southern United Kingdom.

Rain falls all through the year. Sometimes it rains hard. But often, a light mist or steady drizzle falls. The frequent rain gives the valleys a lush, green look. Britain rarely has long stretches of hot, sunny days.

Gray clouds and drizzle pass over this farmhouse in Scotland.

11

Long-Ago Britain

People have lived in the modern-day United Kingdom for thousands of years. The Celts and other groups came to the islands from Europe. They set up clans and kingdoms. At times, outsiders took over parts of the country. The Romans came from Italy. Angles and Saxons attacked from Germany. Lastly, the Normans from France entered.

In the 1500s, England ruled Wales and Ireland. Scotland ruled itself. Scottish and English forces often fought each other. But neither kingdom was able to take over the other—at least not for long.

Boudicca

Boudicca was a Celtic queen. She lived about two thousand years ago. After her husband died, the powerful Romans claimed his kingdom. Boudicca and her forces attacked the Romans. But the Celts lost their fight. Boudicca came to stand for being brave while facing a powerful enemy.

Bamburgh Castle was built on the shores of northern England. It was used for protection against England's invaders for centuries.

Becoming United

How did Britain become united? Wars didn't work. But family ties did. The English queen Elizabeth I didn't have any children. So the kingdom went to her cousin, James, in 1603. But he was also the king of Scotland. For a while, the two kingdoms stayed separate. In the early 1700s, a law united the two. They became the United Kingdom of Great Britain.

Queen Elizabeth I ruled England for forty-five years, from 1558 until her death in 1603.

At the same time, the people of Ireland were trying to end British rule. They tried for two hundred years. By the early 1900s, most of Ireland ruled itself. But the northeastern part of Ireland stayed tied to Britain. In 1921, Britain changed its name to the United Kingdom of Great Britain and Northern Ireland.

In 1886, a law was passed that said Northern Ireland was not allowed to rule itself. Angry protesters attacked British police.

Modern Britain

The United Kingdom once ruled lands called colonies. A colony is land ruled by a faraway country. Britain had colonies throughout the world. They made up the huge British Empire. Over time, most of the colonies became free of British rule. These days, there is no British Empire. But who rules Britain? The British Parliament makes laws for the whole nation.

The Royal Family

Britain still has kings and queens. But they don't rule the country anymore. The country's queen is Elizabeth II. She has been queen for more than fifty years! Her oldest son, Prince Charles, will probably take her place someday. Then he would become King Charles.

Queen Elizabeth II and her son Prince Charles

The British Parliament gathers to hear Queen Elizabeth II speak.

The British People

For hundreds of years, Britain's people were made up of only a few ethnic groups. Most of them had lived in the country for a long time. The Celts are still the major ethnic group in Wales, Scotland, and Northern Ireland. The people of England have Anglo-Saxon and Norman roots.

People gather at Trafalgar Square in London, England.

The old British Empire had ties to countries in Asia, Africa, the Caribbean, and the Pacific. These ties have brought new ethnic groups to the United Kingdom. People from India, Hong Kong, Nigeria, Jamaica, and Australia live in many cities of the United Kingdom.

How Many People?

More than 61 million people live in Britain. England has the most people. It is also the largest part of the United Kingdom. Scotland comes next. Wales is third in size and population. Northern Ireland is the smallest.

Students with long-ago African ties wait for a bus in London.

Biscuits and Bonnets, Lorries and Loos

English is the United Kingdom's official language. But British English uses many different words than American English. Cookies in British English are biscuits. A bonnet is the hood of a car. Trucks are lorries. And a bathroom is a loo. Got it?

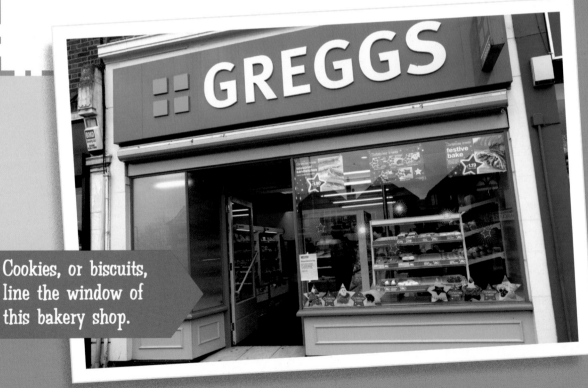

Cookies, or biscuits, line the window of this bakery shop.

Different areas of the country have different accents. An accent is a way of saying words. Some people in Wales, Scotland, and Northern Ireland speak the old languages of Welsh and Gaelic.

Britishisms

American English	British English
principal	head teacher
line up	queue up
sweater	jumper
sneakers	trainers
ballpoint pen	biro
eraser	rubber

This sign is written in both English and Gaelic words.

The Thames River runs through the city of London.

City Life

Nine out of ten people in Britain live in a city or town. Some of the cities are huge! London is the national capital. And it's the United Kingdom's largest city. London sits along the Thames River in southeastern England. Birmingham is another big city. It lies in the Midlands, in the center of England.

Scotland, Wales, and Northern Ireland have their own capital cities. They are all near waterways. Edinburgh, in southeastern Scotland, sits by the Firth of Forth. That's a sea channel of Scotland's Forth River. Cardiff, in southern Wales, lies along the Bristol Channel. Belfast, on the Lagan River, is in the eastern part of Northern Ireland.

More Big Cities

In the 1700s and 1800s, Britain's northern cities were filled with factories. They made goods of wool, metal, and pottery. The goods were brought to port cities in England and Scotland. Ships delivered the goods around the world.

The city of Edinburgh, Scotland, is surrounded by green, rolling hills.

Charming stone cottages and colorful English gardens brighten up the English countryside.

Country Life

Britain has thousands of small villages. Stone cottages line old streets. They sit near old churches and village squares. Villages aren't home to many people. But they offer quiet places to visit and spend free time.

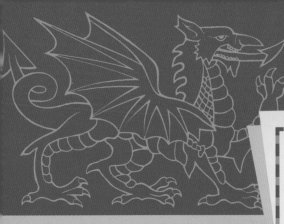

A Welsh Village

Llanfairpwllgwyngyllgogerychwyrndrobwllllantysiliogogogoch is the longest place name in the British Isles. In the Welsh language, the name means "The Church of Mary in the hollow of the white hazel near the fierce whirlpool and the Church of Tysilio by the red cave." Whew!

The train station in the Welsh village with the longest name needs an extra-wide sign.

Getting Around

The British get around in cars and on buses, trains, and subways. Major roads are called motorways. Many were built on the same roads that the Romans built two thousand years ago!

Keeping Left

The British drive on the left side of the road. This rule came from the days of horse-drawn carts and wagons. Drivers held the horse's reins with the left hand. That kept the right hand free for using a sword! Keeping left became the law in 1835.

Motorists in Glasgow, Scotland (*above*), drive on the left. U.S. motorists drive on the right.

London's subway is nicknamed the Tube. It was the first subway ever built. The Tube serves not only London but also nearby towns. Glasgow is the only other United Kingdom city that has subways.

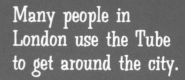

Many people in London use the Tube to get around the city.

Celebrating, British Style

Britain's people celebrate many holidays. Christmas lasts for twelve days. It begins on Christmas Day, December 25. It ends on January 5. In June, locals and tourists alike enjoy watching Trooping the Color. This parade takes place in London. Red-coated soldiers show off their colors (flags).

Bonfire Night

Bonfire Night is November 5. This holiday began in 1605. On that day, an angry group tried to blow up the Houses of Parliament in London. Kids love the bonfires and fireworks that remind people of the event.

Scotland has an August festival called the Edinburgh Military Tattoo. Scottish bagpipers and drummers play their instruments while marching. Watch your step!

Let's Eat

British families often eat cereal for breakfast. A sandwich is a common lunch. Dinner is the main meal of the day. Families try out dishes with pasta or rice, meat, fish, and vegetables. An Indian spice called curry sometimes flavors the food.

A family of four enjoys a meal together at home.

30

Unusual Eats

Some Scottish people like haggis (*left*). Think of haggis as a large sausage. A sheep's heart, lungs, and liver are chopped and mixed with oatmeal, fat, onions, and spices. The mixture is then stuffed into a thin casing and boiled for several hours.

On Sundays at midday, families might have a traditional meal. It features a roast of beef, lamb, or pork. Vegetables are served, along with potatoes covered in gravy. Yorkshire pudding is another favorite part of Sunday lunch. It's not at all like pudding in the United States. Yorkshire pudding is more like a pastry!

School

British kids start school at about the age of five. They are in primary or junior school until the age of eleven. Then they move on to secondary school. They stay there until the age of sixteen. Schools are divided into years instead of grades. So eight- or nine-year-old kids are in year four. This matches U.S. third grade.

Primary students in Scotland work on a lesson with their teacher.

The school year runs from September to July. British kids get breaks of one or two weeks throughout the year. Some kids live at their school. But most kids go to schools close to home.

In the Lab

British kids must learn hi-tech skills throughout their years in school. Most classrooms have an interactive whiteboard. Many schools have computer labs. In the lab, kids practice writing, math, science, and design skills.

These kids in Wales work together on a project.

Green Up!

British kids are finding ways to help the environment. They take part in Earth Day activities. They learn how to save energy. Instead of throwing away old books and toys, they give them to others. They remind their parents to use cloth bags while shopping instead of plastic or paper bags.

By recycling cans, this girl does her part to help keep the United Kingdom green.

Attendants at a festival in Glastonbury, England, show a sign about protecting Earth's climate.

Generation Green

The British website www.generationgreen.co.uk has tons of ideas about how to go green. Games test how much kids know about being a friend to the environment. A fun photo gallery shows projects United Kingdom students have done to help the planet.

Soccer and Cricket

Soccer is called football in Britain. It is the most popular sport. Boys and girls play soccer at school. Entire families root for their favorite professional teams. Rivalries between fans can be noisy! Some of the most famous teams are Chelsea, Manchester United, and Liverpool.

Wayne Rooney (*in red*) of Manchester United gets by a Chelsea player (*in blue*) to score a goal.

Britain's national sport is cricket. This sport reminds some people of baseball. Young and old alike join in. Two teams of eleven people play on large, grassy fields. Families often enjoy a picnic as they watch the action.

Other Sports

Sports such as golf, tennis, and rugby got their start in Britain. Scotland is known as the home of golf. But Northern Ireland and England also have many great golf courses. Tennis fans know the Wimbledon tournament outside London. It draws the world's top players. And Welsh rugby fans cheer their national rugby union team. It has won many international matches.

Just for Fun

What do British kids do for fun? Some play or watch sports, such as soccer, cricket, or tennis. Some belong to the Cub Scouts or Brownies. Britain also has clubs that focus on dance or martial arts. Skateboarding and cycling are popular too. British kids love playing computer games. On the weekends, families sometimes go to the country.

A group of British girls gathers for a Brownie celebration.

Theme Parks

Millions of British people have fun at theme parks. The biggest park is at Pleasure Beach Blackpool. It's in northwestern England. Its roller coasters—including the Big One and Infusion—are fast and furious.

Dear Aunt Mary:

We just came back from a theme park called Alton Towers. Dad said to tell you it's built on land once owned by the earls of Shrewsbury. The coolest part was the roller coasters. I went on Oblivion. It drops straight down. During the ride on Nemesis, I was upside down! The rides were awesome!

Love,
Robert

Alton Towers

The Telly

In Britain, both the young and the old watch a lot of television. Most families have at least one telly. That's what the British call TVs. On average, people watch about twenty-five hours of TV a week. Five main channels offer kids' programs. Other programs include dramas, comedies, sports, and news. The British also have shows about animals, cooking, and gardening.

A family enjoys watching the telly together.

Britain's Got Talent

Since 2007, the show *Britain's Got Talent* has been on TV. Talented kids and adults sing, dance, or play music. They compete to see who's the most talented. In 2008, fourteen-year-old George Sampson *(right)* won on the show. He's a break-dancer. Diversity, a young dance group, won in 2009. Who knows what new stars will appear next?

Britain's Got Talent winner George Sampson shows a break-dancing move at a movie premiere.

41

The Arts

Britain has a long history of great writing, painting, and music. J. K. Rowling is a British author you've probably heard of. British kids love her Harry Potter series. But in school, kids also read the works of famous British authors such as William Shakespeare and Jane Austen.

J. K. Rowling wrote the popular Harry Potter series of books about a boy wizard.

Bands such as the Beatles brought Britain worldwide fame. Later groups, such as the Clash, the Smiths, and Blur, boosted the popularity of punk and alternative rock.

Lads from Liverpool

The Beatles were a band of four guys from Liverpool. They had a cool rock-and-roll sound, shaggy hair, and a sense of fun. They became the hottest band of the 1960s. The Beatles were the start of the "British Invasion." This was a time when British ideas about fashion, art, and music became very popular in the United States.

British band Coldplay performs at a concert to raise money for the victims of the 2010 earthquake in the Caribbean nation of Haiti.

THE FLAG OF THE UNITED KINGDOM

The flag of the United Kingdom is red, white, and blue. Its nickname is the Union Jack. The Union Jack brings together the flags of the country's kingdoms. For an easy way to see all these flags pulled together, go to http://www.woodlands-junior.kent.sch.uk/geography/unionjack.html.

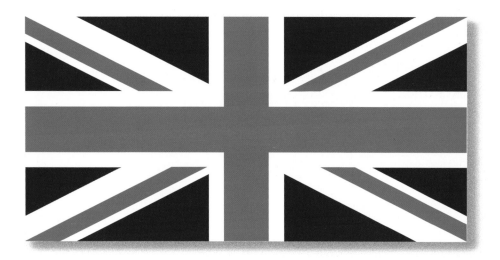

FAST FACTS

FULL COUNTRY NAME: United Kingdom of Great Britain and Northern Ireland

AREA: 94,214 square miles (244,014 square kilometers), or a bit smaller than the state of Oregon

MAIN LANDFORMS:

England: highlands (the Pennines), fertile plains, lowlands, marsh (the Fens), moors, cliffs, valleys, rolling hills

Scotland: highlands (Northwest Highlands, Grampian Mountains), central lowlands, southern uplands, islands (Shetlands, Orkneys, Inner and Outer Hebrides)

Wales: Cambrian Mountains, coastal lowlands, river valleys

Northern Ireland: plains, the mountain ranges Sperrin and Mourne; Antrim Hills; Rathlin and other small islands

MAJOR RIVERS: Thames, Severn, Trent, Ouse (England); Clyde, Tay (Scotland); Lagan, Upper Bann, Lower Bann (Northern Ireland); Dee (Wales)

ANIMALS AND THEIR HABITATS: red deer (Scottish Highlands); roe deer (forests); polecats (forests of Wales, southwestern England); Irish hare (lowlands of Northern Ireland); badgers and foxes (lowlands); puffins (coasts of Scotland, Northern Ireland)

CAPITAL CITY: London

OFFICIAL LANGUAGE: English

POPULATION: about 61,300,000

GLOSSARY

British Empire: a large group of lands around the world that Britain once ruled

capital: a city where the government of a state or country is located

clan: a large group of families who share a common ancestor

colony: a land that a foreign country rules from far away

ethnic group: a group of people with many things in common, such as language, religion, and customs

goods: things to sell

interactive whiteboard: a display screen that is linked to a computer and projector. Students interact with the board by using tools called responders.

island: a piece of land surrounded by water

map: a drawing or chart of all or part of Earth or the sky

mountain: a part of Earth's surface that rises high into the sky

port: an area on the shore of a body of water where ships can load and unload goods safely

subway: an underground train that moves large numbers of people quickly

valley: an area of low land

TO LEARN MORE

BOOKS

Limke, Jeff. *King Arthur: Excalibur Unsheathed*. New York: Graphic Universe, 2007. This graphic novel tells the story of how Arthur pulled a sword out of a stone to become king of England.

MacDonald, Margaret Reed. *The Great Smelly, Slobbery, Small-Tooth Dog: A Folktale from Great Britain*. Atlanta: August House, 2007. This fun retelling takes the story of Beauty and the Beast into new territory.

Sasek, Miroslav. *This Is Britain*. New York: Universe Publishing, 2008. Classic illustrations and lively text introduce Britain and its most famous sights.

Welby, Rebecca. *Hello Britain!* London: Beautiful Books, 2006. This clever book gives kids tasks to perform to find out how "British" they are. A website posts the results.

WEBSITES

Enchanted Learning
http://www.enchantedlearning.com/geography
This site has pages of Britain and its flag to label and color.

Time for Kids
http://www.timeforkids.com/TFK/kids/hh/goplaces/main/0,28375,604850,00.html
This site tells all about England, part of the United Kingdom of Great Britain and Northern Ireland. It includes a virtual tour of England, a fun quiz you can try, and e-cards you can send to family and friends.

INDEX